THE ANALECTS OF CONFUCIUS
A SELECTION
CHINESE-ENGLISH

論語精選

漢語－英語對照

U0641140

主 編: 陳 虎
Editor-in-Chief: Chen Hu

翻 譯: 楊 彬
Translator: Yang Bin

審 校: 王 卓
Reviewer: Wang Zhuo

山東教育出版社 ·濟南·
Shandong Education Press ·Jinan·

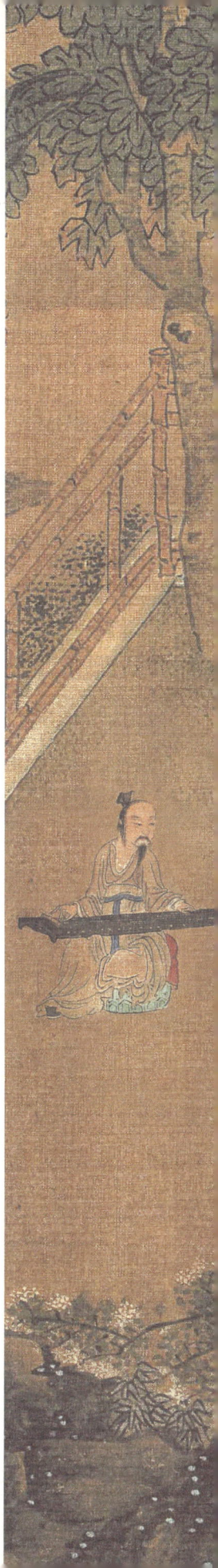

圖書在版編目（CIP）數據

論語精選 ： 漢語、英語對照 / 陳虎主編. -- 濟南：
山東教育出版社， 2024. 9. -- ISBN 978-7-5701-3242-3

Ⅰ. B222.21

中國國家版本館CIP數據核字第2024ZK3463號

責任編輯：岳思聰
責任校對：劉　園
整體設計：閆　姝　吳江楠

LUNYU JINGXUAN: HANYU–YINGYU DUIZHAO

論語精選：漢語－英語對照

主管單位：山東出版傳媒股份有限公司
出版發行：山東教育出版社
地　　址：濟南市市中區二環南路2066號4區1號　　　郵編：250003
電　　話：0531-82092660　　　　網址：www.sjs.com.cn
印　　刷：山東華立印務有限公司
開本規格：787 mm×1092 mm　1/16
印　　張：10
字　　數：112千
版　　次：2024年9月第1版
印　　次：2024年9月第1次印刷
定　　價：398.00元

（如印裝質量有問題，請與印刷廠聯系調換）
電　　話：0634-6216033

目录
Contents

第一章

Chapter I　Learning

爲學

一

子曰：『學而時習之，不亦説乎？有朋自遠方來，不亦樂乎？人不知而不愠，不亦君子乎？』

二

子曰：『君子食無求飽，居無求安，敏於事而慎於言，就有道而正焉，可謂好學也已。』

1

Confucius said, "Is it not a joy to learn and, in due time, apply what has been learned? Is it not a delight to receive friends coming from afar? Is it not the mark of the gentleman to remain unperturbed when his virtues go unacknowledged?"

2

Confucius said, "The gentleman does not seek to satisfy his appetite fully; nor does he demand comfort in his dwelling. He is diligent in what he is doing and cautious in his speech. He seeks to improve himself by learning from those who are virtuous. Thus, he can be said to be fond of learning."

三
二

子曰：『吾十有五而志于學，三十而立，四十而不惑，五十而知天命，六十而耳順，七十而從心所欲，不踰矩。』

子曰：『溫故而知新，可以爲師矣。』

子曰：『學而不思則罔，思而不學則殆。』

3

Confucius said, "At fifteen, I set my heart upon learning. At thirty, I had planted my feet firmly on the path of propriety. At forty, I became free of doubts about anything I undertook. At fifty, I knew the decrees of Heaven. At sixty, I could discern truth from falsehood and right from wrong upon hearing others speak. At seventy, I could follow my heart's desires without transgressing the bounds of virtuous conduct."

Confucius said, "If one keeps reviewing what he has learned and gains new understanding and insights, he can be a teacher of others."

Confucius said, "Studying without thinking is futile while thinking without studying is dangerous."

四

子曰：『不憤不啟，不悱不發。舉一隅不以三隅反，則不復也。』

子曰：『我非生而知之者，好古，敏以求之者也。』

子曰：『三人行，必有我師焉，擇其善者而從之，其不善者而改之。』

4

Confucius said, "I do not guide a student until he desires to understand but cannot find an answer. I do not inspire him until he wishes to speak but cannot put an idea into words. If I teach him one aspect of a matter and he cannot draw inferences about the others, I will not repeat my lesson."

Confucius said, "I am not one who was born with knowledge; I am one who loves the ancient culture and earnestly strives to acquire it."

Confucius said, "When I walk in a group of people, there must be one I can learn from. I would choose their merits to follow and their imperfections to correct."

五

六

七

子曰：『學如不及，猶恐失之。』

子曰：『古之學者爲己，今之學者爲人。』

子曰：『吾嘗終日不食，終夜不寢，以思，無益，不如學也。』

5

Confucius said, "Learn as if you'll never be able to catch up with everything you need to know and as if you're afraid you'll lose everything that you've already gained."

6

Confucius said, "Ancient scholars engaged in learning to cultivate themselves. Modern scholars engage in learning to adorn themselves for others to see."

7

Confucius said, "I once spent a whole day without food and a whole night without sleep just for pondering, but I gained nothing from it. It would have been better to devote that time to learning."

八

孔子曰：『生而知之者上也，學而知之者次也。困而學之，又其次也。困而不學，民斯爲下矣。』

九

子曰：『小子何莫學夫詩？詩，可以興，可以觀，可以羣，可以怨。邇之事父，遠之事君，多識於鳥獸草木之名。』

十

子夏曰：『日知其所亡，月無忘其所能，可謂好學也已矣。』

8

Confucius said, "Those who are born with knowledge are the best; those who acquire knowledge by study are the next; those who, when encountering problems, learn and acquire knowledge are tertiary; and those who, when encountering problems, still refuse to learn are of the lowest order."

9

Confucius said, "Young men, why do you not study the *Book of Songs*? The *Book of Songs* can enrich your imagination, provide a vehicle for contemplation, help you to interact with others, and voice a complaint more effectively. At home it teaches you how to serve your parents; further afield it teaches you how to serve the prince. Additionally, it helps you gain knowledge of birds, beasts, plants and trees."

10

Zixia said, "To learn something new every day and to review what has been learned every month can be considered as being diligent in learning."

第二章

Chapter II　Humaneness

仁

一

子曰：『巧言令色，鮮矣仁！』

二

子曰：『我未見好仁者，惡不仁者。好仁者，無以尚之；惡不仁者，其為仁矣，不使不仁者加乎其身。有能一日用其力於仁矣乎？我未見力不足者。蓋有之矣，我未之見也。』

1

Confucius said, "Those who speak with flowery words and display a facade of hypocrisy do not possess much humaneness."

2

Confucius said, "I have never seen a person who truly loved humaneness or a person who was truly repelled by the lack of humaneness. A person who truly loved humaneness would think that nothing could surpass humaneness. A person who was truly repelled by the lack of humaneness, while putting humaneness into practice, would not allow any inhumane person to influence his conduct. Is it possible for a person, in the space of a day, to devote all his effort to the practice of humaneness? I have never seen a person who lacks the strength to do so. There may be one, but I have not seen such a person."

四

三

子貢曰：『如有博施於民而能濟衆，何如？可謂仁乎？』子曰：『何事於仁，必也聖乎！堯、舜其猶病諸。夫仁者，己欲立而立人，己欲達而達人。能近取譬，可謂仁之方也已。』

曾子曰：『士不可以不弘毅，任重而道遠。仁以爲己任，不亦重乎？死而後已，不亦遠乎？』

3

Zigong asked, "If there is someone who generously bestows benefits upon people and helps everyone live well, can he be called humane?" Confucious replied, "It's more than humaneness. It would be a sage's virtue! Even Yao and Shun might have found it difficult to achieve such a feat. What is humaneness? A humane person wishes to establish himself, and so he helps others to establish themselves. He wishes to reach his goal, and so he helps others to reach theirs. To take examples from oneself and apply them to others might be a way of realizing humaneness."

4

Zengzi said, "A scholar must be resolute and persevering, for his burden is heavy and his journey is long. To take on the responsibility of practicing humaneness throughout the world, is that not a heavy burden? To strive for it until the end of one's life, is that not a long journey?"

五

顏淵問仁。子曰：『克己復禮爲仁。一日克己復禮，天下歸仁焉。爲仁由己，而由人乎哉？』

顏淵曰：『請問其目。』子曰：『非禮勿視，非禮勿聽，非禮勿言，非禮勿動。』

顏淵曰：『回雖不敏，請事斯語矣。』

5

Yan Yuan asked about humaneness. Confucius said, "To restrain yourself and make your words and actions conform to the rules of propriety is the way to be humane. Once you achieve this, people throughout the world will acknowledge you as a humane person. Practicing humaneness depends solely on yourself, not on others."

Yan Yuan asked, "I would like to know the guiding principles for action." Confucius said, "Do not look at anything nor listen to anything nor speak of anything nor do anything against the rules of propriety."

Yan Yuan said, "Dull as I am, I would strive to put into practice what you have said."

仲弓問仁。子曰：『出門如見大賓，使民如承大祭。己所不欲，勿施於人。在邦無怨，在家無怨。』

仲弓曰：『雍雖不敏，請事斯語矣。』

Zhonggong asked about humaneness. Confucius said, "Going out to work is like receiving an esteemed guest; managing the people is like handling a great sacrificial ceremony. In both, you must be serious and meticulous. Do not impose on others what you yourself do not desire. If you do not harbor resentment in your work, then even when you are off duty, you will not harbor resentment."

Zhonggong said, "Dull as I am, I would strive to put into practice what you have said."

六

樊遲問仁。子曰：『愛人。』問知。子曰：『知人。』

樊遲未達。子曰：『舉直錯諸枉，能使枉者直。』

樊遲退，見子夏曰：『鄉也吾見於夫子而問知，子曰：「舉直錯諸枉，能使枉者直。」何謂也？』

子夏曰：『富哉言乎！舜有天下，選於眾，舉皋陶，不仁者遠矣。湯有天下，選於眾，舉伊尹，不仁者遠矣。』

6

Fan Chi asked about humaneness. Confucius said, "Love others." He then asked about wisdom. Confucius said, "Know others."

Fan Chi did not fully understand. Confucius explained further, "Promote the upright and place them over the wicked, which can make the wicked upright."

Fan Chi withdrew and found Zixia, saying, "Just now, I went to see the Master and asked him about wisdom. He said, 'Promote the upright and place them over the wicked.' What does that mean?"

Zixia replied, "What a profound statement! When Shun was emperor, he selected Gao Yao and put him in charge, then those who were without humaneness disappeared. When Tang was emperor, he selected and promoted Yi Yin, then those who were without humaneness stayed away."

七

樊遲問仁。子曰：『居處恭，執事敬，與人忠。雖之夷狄，不可棄也。』

八

子曰：『剛、毅、木、訥近仁。』

子曰：『志士仁人，無求生以害仁，有殺身以成仁。』

7

Fan Chi asked about humaneness. Confucius said, "Maintain a dignified and solemn demeanor in daily life, work with seriousness and diligence, and serve others with sincerity and devotion. These virtues should not be abandoned, even when you go to a foreign land."

Confucius said, "To be resolute, decisive, simple, and cautious in speech—those who possess these four qualities are close to humaneness."

8

Confucius said, "The men of noble aspirations and virtue would not seek to stay alive at the expense of humaneness. They might even sacrifice their lives to have humaneness fulfilled."

十　　九

子張問仁於孔子。孔子曰：『能行五者於天下，爲仁矣。』
『請問之。』曰：『恭，寬，信，敏，惠。恭則不侮，寬則得衆，信則人任焉，
敏則有功，惠則足以使人。』

子夏曰：『博學而篤志，切問而近思，仁在其中矣。』

9

Zizhang asked Confucius about humaneness. Confucius said, "One who can practice Five Virtues in all aspects of life is a man of humaneness."

Zizhang asked, "What are the Five Virtues?" Confucius said, "Dignity, leniency, sincerity, diligence, and generosity. Dignity prevents one from being insulted. Leniency gains the support of the people. Sincerity leads to being entrusted with responsibilities. Diligence ensures high efficiency and great contributions. Generosity enables one to command others."

10

Zixia said, "To learn extensively and adhere to aspirations, to inquire earnestly, and reflect on things close at hand—this is where humaneness lies."

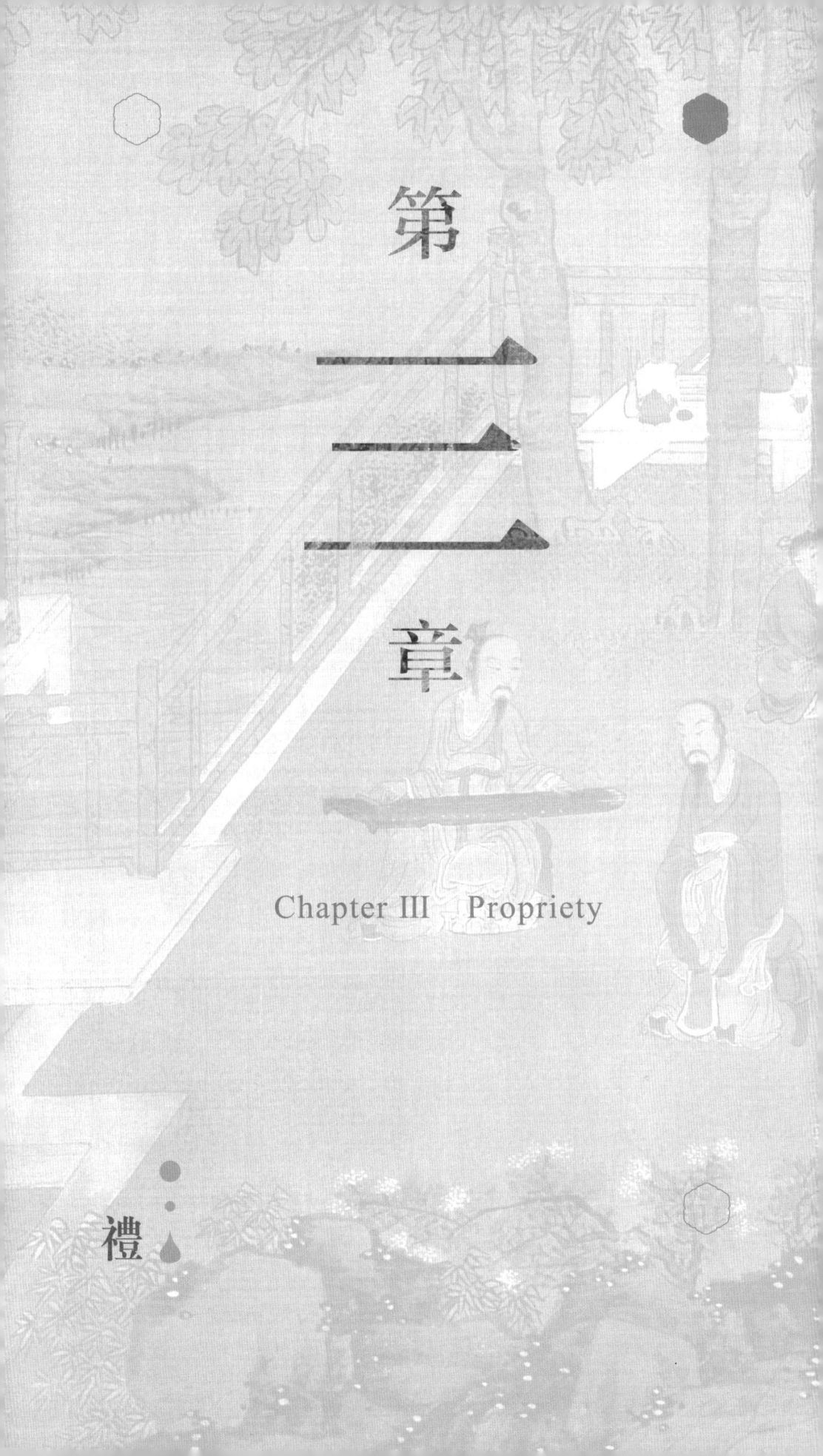

第三章

Chapter III Propriety

禮

一

　　有子曰：『禮之用，和爲貴。先王之道，斯爲美；小大由之。有所不行，知和而和，不以禮節之，亦不可行也。』

二

　　子張問：『十世可知也？』子曰：『殷因於夏禮，所損益，可知也；周因於殷禮，所損益，可知也。其或繼周者，雖百世，可知也。』

1

Youzi said, "Harmony is what is most prized in the Rites. This was the precious aspect of governance by the virtuous rulers of the past. They handled both minor and major affairs in a harmonious way. However, if there are instances where it is not feasible to do so, to pursue harmony for its own sake without being regulated by established norms and rules is not advisable."

2

Zizhang asked Confucius, "Could the rites and institutions of the next ten generations be known in advance?" Confucius said, "The Shang Dynasty followed the ritual system of the Xia Dynasty; what was abolished and what was added could be known. The Zhou Dynasty followed the ritual system of the preceding Shang Dynasty; what was abolished and what was added could also be known. Therefore, what continues from the Zhou Dynasty, even for the next hundred generations, could be foreseen."

三

林放問禮之本。子曰：『大哉問！禮，與其奢也，寧儉；喪，與其易也，寧戚。』

子夏問曰：『巧笑倩兮，美目盼兮，素以爲絢兮。』何謂也？」子曰：『繪事後素。』

曰：『禮後乎？』子曰：『起予者商也！始可與言《詩》已矣。』

子曰：『夏禮，吾能言之，杞不足徵也；殷禮，吾能言之，宋不足徵也。文獻不足故也。足，則吾能徵之矣。』

Lin Fang (a man of the state of Lu) asked about the essence of the Rites. Confucius said, "A significant question indeed! Regarding general rites, it is better to be simple and frugal than to be extravagant. Concerning funeral rites, it is better to express genuine sorrow excessively than to observe the formalities meticulously."

Zixia asked Confucius, "'How beautiful is the smiling face with its dimples, how charming the bright eyes that glance about, and how pure the white ground covered with flowers?' What does this poem mean?" Confucius said, "The white ground must first be prepared before the flowers are painted."

Zixia asked, "So, does this imply that the origins of the Rites and Music come after humaneness and righteousness?" Confucius said, "You are really someone who can inspire me. Now we can discuss the *Book of Songs* together."

Confucius said, "I can speak of the Rites of the Xia Dynasty, but its descendant State of Qi is not able to provide evidence to support what I say. I can speak of the Rites of the Shang Dynasty, but its descendant State of Song is not able to provide evidence to support what I say. This is because both the records and worthy men of erudition are insufficient in these two states. If they were plentiful, I could support my words with evidence."

四

定公問：『君使臣，臣事君，如之何？』孔子對曰：『君使臣以禮，臣事君以忠。』

五

子曰：『能以禮讓爲國乎？何有？不能以禮讓爲國，如禮何？』

4

Prince Ding of Lu asked Confucius, "How should a prince employ his ministers, and how should ministers serve their prince?" Confucius replied, "A prince should employ his ministers according to the Rites, and ministers should serve their prince with loyalty."

5

Confucius said, "Is it possible to govern a state by observing the Rites and showing deference? What would be difficult about that? If one fails to accomplish this, then how can he deal with the rituals?"

六

子曰：『恭而無禮則勞，慎而無禮則葸，勇而無禮則亂，直而無禮則絞。君子篤於親，則民興於仁；故舊不遺，則民不偷。』

七

子曰：『麻冕，禮也；今也純，儉，吾從眾。拜下，禮也；今拜乎上，泰也。雖違眾，吾從下。』

6

Confucius said, "To focus on a dignified appearance and manner without understanding propriety leads to exhaustion. To be overly cautious without understanding propriety leads to timidity. To act boldly without understanding propriety leads to recklessness. To speak frankly without understanding propriety can be sharp and rude. When those in high positions treat their family and kin with deep affection, the people will tend towards humaneness. When those in high positions do not abandon their old colleagues and friends, the people will not be indifferent towards others."

7

Confucius said, "The Rites prescribed that a sacrificial cap should be made of linen. Today, people use a silk one instead, which is more frugal. I agree with the current practice. When a minister meets the sovereign, he should first bow on the steps below the hall, and then do it again after ascending the hall. This conforms to the Rites. Nowadays, people omit the bow on the steps and only do it after ascending the hall, which is a manifestation of arrogance. Although it goes against the current practice, I still advocate bowing on the steps before ascending the hall."

八

子曰：『博學於文，約之以禮，亦可以弗畔矣夫！』

九

孔子曰：『天下有道，則禮樂征伐自天子出；天下無道，則禮樂征伐自諸侯出。自諸侯出，蓋十世希不失矣；自大夫出，五世希不失矣；陪臣執國命，三世希不失矣。天下有道，則政不在大夫。天下有道，則庶人不議。』

8

Confucius said, "The gentleman extensively studies the classics and then restrains himself with propriety, thereby avoiding deviation from the path of righteousness."

9

Confucius said, "When good government reigns, the Rites, Music and military campaigns are all initiated by the Son of Heaven. When bad government reigns, the Rites, Music and military campaigns are all initiated by princes. In this case, it is very rare that power is maintained beyond ten generations. If the Rites, Music and military campaigns are all initiated by ministers, it is very rare that power is maintained beyond five generations. If the state political power is held by the subsidiary ministers, it is rarely maintained beyond three generations. If good government reigns, power would not be lost into the hands of ministers. Likewise, if good government reigns, common folks will not be fond of political discussions among themselves."

十

二

孔子曰：『不知命，無以爲君子也；不知禮，無以立也；不知言，無以知人也。』

10

Confucius said, "Without understanding destiny, one cannot be regarded as a true gentleman; without understanding propriety, one cannot stand firm in society; without understanding how to discern others' words, one cannot truly know people."

第

四

章

Chapter IV　Wisdom

知

一

子曰：『由！誨女知之乎！知之爲知之，不知爲不知，是知也。』

二

子曰：『里仁爲美。擇不處仁，焉得知？』

子曰：『不仁者不可以久處約，不可以長處樂。仁者安仁，知者利仁。』

1

Confucius said, "Zhong You, let me teach you the right attitude towards knowledge and ignorance. To hold what you know and admit what you do not know, that is true wisdom."

2

Confucius said, "What makes a neighborhood excellent and beautiful is its abundance of virtue. How can it be called wise if one chooses to reside in a neighborhood without true virtue?"

Confucius said, "A person who is not humane cannot endure adversity or enjoy happiness for long. A humane person feels at home in humaneness. A wise person practices it because he sees benefits in humaneness."

三

二

子曰：『臧文仲居蔡，山節藻梲，何如其知也？』

子曰：『寧武子，邦有道，則知；邦無道，則愚。其知可及也，其愚不可及也。』

四

二

樊遲問知。子曰：『務民之義，敬鬼神而遠之，可謂知矣。』問仁。曰：『仁者先難而後獲，可謂仁矣。』

子曰：『知者樂水，仁者樂山。知者動，仁者靜。知者樂，仁者壽。』

3

Confucius said, "Zang Wenzhong built a house for a large turtle named Cai, with carved brackets resembling mountains and painted columns adorned with algae patterns. How could such a person be considered wise?"

Confucius said, "When the state is well governed, Ning Wuzi demonstrates his wisdom. When the state is poorly governed, he pretends to be foolish. Others can match his wisdom, but few can match his ability to feign foolishness."

4

Fan Chi asked about the essence of wisdom. Confucius said, "To focus one's efforts on guiding the people towards righteousness, to treat ghosts and spirits with reverence but without intention to approach them, can be considered wisdom." Fan Chi then asked about humaneness. Confucius replied, "The humane person exerts effort first and then reaps the fruits of his labor. This is humaneness."

Confucius said, "The wise find pleasure in water; the humane find pleasure in hills. The wise are active; the humane are tranquil. The wise are joyful; the humane enjoy longevity."

六　五

子貢曰：『夫子自道也。』

子曰：『君子道者三，我無能焉：仁者不憂，知者不惑，勇者不懼。』子

子曰：『知者不惑，仁者不憂，勇者不懼。』

子曰：『吾有知乎哉？無知也。有鄙夫問於我，空空如也。我叩其兩端而竭焉。』

5

Confucius said, "Do I possess knowledge? No, I do not. A farmer once asked me a question, and I knew nothing about it initially. By inquiring about all details of the things in question, I was able to gain some insights and then did my best to inform him."

Confucius said, "The wise are not easily confused, the humane are often optimistic, and the courageous are free from fear."

6

Confucius said, "There are three things that the gentleman practices which I have not yet been able to achieve: The wise are not easily confused, the humane are often optimistic, and the courageous are free from fear." Zigong said, "The Master has just given a description of himself."

七

二

子路問成人。子曰：『若臧武仲之知，公綽之不欲，卞莊子之勇，冉求之藝，文之以禮樂，亦可以爲成人矣。』

7

Zilu asked how to define the perfect man. Confucius said, "To have the wisdom of Zang Wuzhong, the purity and self-restraint of Meng Gongchuo, the bravery of Bian Zhuangzi, the versatility of Ran Qiu, and literary refinement cultivated by the Rites and Music—one who possesses all these qualities can be considered a perfect man."

八

二

子曰：『可與言而不與之言，失人；不可與言而與之言，失言。知者不失人，亦不失言。』

子曰：『知及之，仁不能守之；雖得之，必失之。知及之，仁能守之，不莊以涖之，則民不敬。知及之，仁能守之，莊以涖之，動之不以禮，未善也』。

子曰：『君子不可小知，而可大受也；小人不可大受，而可小知也』。』

8

Confucius said, "When you should talk to someone but do not, it is a missed opportunity for talent. When you should not talk to someone but do so, it is a waste of words. A man of wisdom would neither miss opportunities for talent nor waste words."

Confucius said, "If one's wisdom is sufficient to obtain power, but he lacks the virtue to maintain it, he will certainly lose it. If one possesses both wisdom and virtue and maintains what he has obtained, governing the people without sincerity and carnestness will lead the people to not take their lives and work seriously. Even if one has the knowledge and virtue to obtain and maintain power, and governs with sincerity and earnestness, yet he does not follow the Rites while employing the service of the people, that will not work either."

Confucius said, "The gentleman should not be tested with trivial matters but can be entrusted with important commissions. The petty man should not undertake important tasks but can be tested with trivial matters."

九

一

陽貨欲見孔子，孔子不見，歸孔子豚。

孔子時其亡也，而往拜之。

遇諸塗。

謂孔子曰：『來！予與爾言。』曰：『懷其寶而迷其邦，可謂仁乎？』

曰：『不可。好從事而亟失時，可謂知乎？』曰：『不可。日月逝矣，歲

不我與。』

孔子曰：『諾。吾將仕矣。』

9

Yang Huo wanted Confucius to visit him, but Confucius did not go. So, Yang Huo sent Confucius a steamed piglet as a present to make Confucius come to his house to express thanks.

Confucius waited until he heard that Yang was not at home and then went to offer his thanks.

However, he met Yang Huo on the way.

Yang Huo called out to Confucius, "Come! I want to talk to you." Confucius approached him. Yang Huo said, "One has talents but stand by while the affairs of the state are in disarray—can this be called humaneness?" Confucius did not respond. Yang answered his own question, "No, it cannot." He continued, "One desires a position but repeatedly misses the opportunities—can this be called wisdom?" Confucius still remained silent. Yang Huo again answered his own question, "No, it cannot." He then continued, "Time will never return once it passes."

Confucius finally said, "Alright, I will consider taking an official position."

十二

陳子禽謂子貢曰：『子爲恭也，仲尼豈賢於子乎？』

子貢曰：『君子一言以爲知，一言以爲不知，言不可不愼也。夫子之不可及也，猶天之不可階而升也。夫子之得邦家者，所謂立之斯立，道之斯行，綏之斯來，動之斯和。其生也榮，其死也哀，如之何其可及也？』

10

Chen Ziqin asked Zigong, "Are you too polite or humble? How could Confucius be more worthy than you?"

Zigong replied, "A gentleman reveals his wisdom or ignorance through his words, so one must be careful with speech. The greatness of my Master is unreachable, just as the heavens cannot be ascended to with a ladder. If he had become a ruler of a state or a minister with a fief, as we believe, the people would find their place in society, progress under his guidance, come together from distant places when reassured, and unite when mobilized. He was honored when he was alive and mourned when he died. Who could possibly match him?"

第

五

章

Chapter V　Trustworthiness

信

一

曾子曰：『吾日三省吾身：爲人謀而不忠乎？與朋友交而不信乎？

傳不習乎？』

二

子曰：『道千乘之國，敬事而信，節用而愛人，使民以時。』

子曰：『弟子，入則孝，出則弟，謹而信，汎愛衆，而親仁。行有餘力，則

以學文。』

1

Zengzi said, "I reflect on myself multiple times every day: Have I done my utmost in serving others? Have I been sincere in my dealings with friends? Have I reviewed and practiced the teachings that my teacher has imparted to me?"

Confucius said, "To govern a big state with a thousand chariots, one must handle affairs with seriousness, honesty and frugality, care for officials, and utilize the labor of the common people during their agricultural off-season."

2

Confucius said, "Young people, when with their parents, should be filial; when away from home, they should respect their elders. They should speak sparingly and sincerely, love the masses and be close to those with virtue. After practicing these principles diligently, if there is still energy left over, they should then study the classics."

四

三

有子曰：『信近於義，言可復也。恭近於禮，遠恥辱也。因不失其親，亦可宗也。』

子曰：『人而無信，不知其可也。大車無輗，小車無軏，其何以行之哉？』

3

Youzi said, "Only when your truthfulness is close to righteousness can you keep a promise; only when your respectfulness is close to propriety can you keep humiliation away; only when you love those akin to you are you worthy of esteem."

4

Confucius said, "If a person does not have the trust of others, I do not know how he can get along. A big cart without the hinge, or a small cart without the pin—how can one make it move forward?"

六

五

顏淵季路侍。子曰：『盍各言爾志？』

子路曰：『願車馬衣輕裘，與朋友共，敝之而無憾。』

顏淵曰：『願無伐善，無施勞。』

子路曰：『願聞子之志。』

子曰：『老者安之，朋友信之，少者懷之。』

子曰：『主忠信，無友不如己者，過則勿憚改。』

5

Confucius was seated, while Yan Yuan and Zilu were standing respectfully by the Master's side. Confucius asked, "Why don't each of you tell me of your aspirations?"

Zilu said, "I would like to share my carriages, horses, and clothes with my friends, and have no complaints if they are worn out or damaged."

Yan Yuan said, "I wish never to boast about my merits, nor to proclaim my accomplishments."

Zilu turned to Confucius and said, "We would like to hear your aspirations."

Confucius replied, "My aspiration is to make the elderly feel secure and comfortable, to gain the trust of my friends, and to be remembered fondly by the young."

6

Confucius said, "You should primarily cultivate the virtues of loyalty and trustworthiness. Do not make friends with those who are less virtuous than yourself. When you have made a mistake, do not hesitate to correct it."

七

二

子貢問曰：『何如斯可謂之士矣？』子曰：『行己有恥，使於四方，不辱君命，可謂士矣。』

曰：『敢問其次。』曰：『宗族稱孝焉，鄉黨稱弟焉。』

曰：『敢問其次。』曰：『言必信，行必果，硜硜然小人哉！抑亦可以為次矣。』

7

Zigong asked, "What makes a person a true scholar-official?" Confucius said, "A person who maintains a sense of humility and fulfills the tasks of his prince when sent on missions abroad can be called a true scholar-official."

Zigong asked, "May I ask what kind of person ranks one step below that?" Confucius said, "One who is praised by his clan for being filial to his parents and by his neighborhood for being respectful to his elders."

Zigong asked again, "May I ask what kind of person may be placed in the next lower rank?" Confucius said, "A person whose word can be trusted and who completes whatever task he undertakes. In his stubborn determination, he may resemble a petty man, and he could still probably qualify as a scholar-official of a lower rank."

九　八

　二

子張問崇德辨惑。子曰：『主忠信，徙義，崇德也。愛之欲其生，惡之欲其死。既欲其生，又欲其死，是惑也。』『誠不以富，亦祇以異。』」

　二

子張問行。子曰：『言忠信，行篤敬，雖蠻貊之邦行矣。言不忠信，行不篤敬，雖州里行乎哉？立則見其參於前也，在輿則見其倚於衡也，夫然後行。』」

8

Zizhang asked how to cultivate virtue and dispel perplexity. Confucious said, "To uphold loyalty and trustworthiness, and to follow righteousness—this is how to cultivate virtue. When you love someone, you wish him to live longer; when you loathe him, you wish him to die soon. To wish him to live at one moment and to wish him to die at the next—this is a case of perplexity. Indeed, it brings no personal benefit, only causing others to wonder."

9

Zizhang asked how one could conduct oneself so as to be successful everywhere. Confucius said, "If one speaks sincerely and honestly and behaves with integrity and dignity, even in a foreign land, one will succeed. But if one speaks deceitfully and behaves harshly and flippantly, even in one's own hometown, how can one succeed? When standing, one should imagine seeing the words 'sincerity, honesty, integrity, and dignity' before one's eyes; in the carriage, one should imagine seeing these words carved on the front beam. Only by constantly keeping these words in mind can one succeed everywhere."

十一

子夏曰：『君子信而後勞其民；未信，則以爲厲己也。信而後諫；未信，則以爲謗己也。』

10

Zixia said, "The gentleman must first gain the trust of the people before mobilizing them; otherwise, the people will think he is oppressing them. He must earn the trust of the prince before offering advice; otherwise, the prince will interpret it as defamation."

第

六

章

Chapter VI　Filial Piety

孝

一

子曰：『父在，觀其志；父沒，觀其行；三年無改於父之道，可謂孝矣。』

二

有子曰：『其爲人也孝弟，而好犯上者，鮮矣；不好犯上，而好作亂者，未之有也。君子務本，本立而道生。孝弟也者，其爲仁之本與！』

1

Confucius said, "While a man's father is alive, observe his aspirations; when his father is dead, examine his conduct. If he maintains the reasonable aspects of his father's ways for a long time without change, it can be said that he has achieved filial piety."

2

Youzi said, "It is rare for someone who is filial to their parents and respectful to their elder brothers to enjoy offending their superiors; there has never been anyone who dislikes offending their superiors but enjoys rebelling. The gentleman concerns himself with the fundamentals. Once the fundamentals are established, the True Way appears. Filial piety and fraternal duty should be the basis of humaneness."

四　　　三

二　　　二

或謂孔子曰：『子奚不爲政？』子曰：『《書》云：「孝乎惟孝，友于兄弟，施於有政。」是亦爲政，奚其爲爲政？』

孟懿子問孝。子曰：『無違。』

樊遲御，子告之曰：『孟孫問孝於我，我對曰：「無違。」』樊遲曰：『何謂也？』子曰：『生，事之以禮；死，葬之以禮，祭之以禮。』

3

Someone asked Confucius, "Why don't you engage in politics?" Confucius replied, "According to the *Book of Documents*, 'By being filial to your parents and being kind to your brothers, you're contributing to the smooth running of the government.' Since I'm already doing this, why must I hold an official position to be considered engaging in politics?"

4

Meng Yizi asked Confucius about filial piety. Confucius said, "Do not violate propriety."

Later, when Fan Chi was driving a carriage for Confucius, Confucius told him, "Meng asked me about filial piety, and I replied that one should not violate propriety." Fan Chi asked, "What did you mean by that?" Confucius replied, "When your parents are alive, serve them in accord with propriety. After they have passed away, bury them and offer sacrifices to them in accord with propriety."

六

五

二

一

二

一

子夏問孝。子曰：『色難。有事，弟子服其勞；有酒食，先生饌，曾是以爲孝乎？』

子游問孝。子曰：『今之孝者，是謂能養。至於犬馬，皆能有養。不敬，何以別乎？』

孟武伯問孝。子曰：『父母唯其疾之憂。』

5

Meng Wubo asked about filial piety. Confucius said, "Give your parents no cause for worry other than your illness."

Ziyou asked about filial piety. Confucius said, "Nowadays, people consider filial piety as merely providing for their parents' basic needs. However, even dogs and horses are provided for. If one does not sincerely show filial piety to his parents, how can he distinguish between providing for his parents and feeding dogs and horses?"

6

Zixia asked about filial piety. Confucius said, "It is difficult for a son to always have a pleasant facial expression in front of his parents. As for the youngsters taking on the burden when there is work to be done and the older ones being served first when there is food and wine, can this be called filial conduct?"

七

一

子曰：『事父母幾諫，見志不從，又敬不違，勞而不怨。』

子曰：『父母在，不遠遊，遊必有方。』

子曰：『三年無改於父之道，可謂孝矣。』

子曰：『父母之年，不可不知也。一則以喜，一則以懼。』

7

Confucius said, "When one serves his parents, if they are in the wrong, one may correct them, but politely. If one sees that they won't take his advice, he should still be respectful, without offending them. He may be concerned, but he should not resent them."

Confucius said, "While one's parents are alive, one should not travel far away. If he does travel, he must have a precise destination."

Confucius said, "If one maintains the reasonable aspects of his father's ways for a long time without change, it can be said that he has achieved filial piety."

Confucius said, "One should always keep in mind the age of his parents. On the one hand, he is pleased with their longevity. On the other hand, he is worried about their decrepitude."

八

子曰：『孝哉閔子騫！人不間於其父母、昆弟之言。』

九

葉公語孔子曰：『吾黨有直躬者，其父攘羊，而子證之。』孔子曰：『吾黨之直者異於是：父爲子隱，子爲父隱。直在其中矣。』

十

曾子曰：『吾聞諸夫子：孟莊子之孝也，其他可能也。其不改父之臣與父之政，是難能也。』

8

Confucius said, "Min Ziqian is truly filial! There is no disagreement among people about the praise his parents and brothers give him."

9

Lord She told Confucius, "In my hometown, there is a righteous man. When his father stole a sheep, he reported him." Confucius said, "In my land, the righteous men are different from this. The fathers would conceal the misdeeds of their sons and the sons would conceal the misdeeds of their fathers. Herein lies righteousness."

10

Zengzi said, "I have heard our Master say, 'The filial piety of Meng Zhuangzi, in other matters, was nothing special. But retaining his father's subordinates and maintaining his father's political institutions was quite difficult for others to emulate.'"

第

七

章

Chapter VII Friendship

友

一

〓〓

子曰：『視其所以，觀其所由，察其所安。人焉廋哉？人焉廋哉？』

二

〓〓

子游曰：『事君數，斯辱矣；朋友數，斯疏矣。』

1

Confucius said, "See the company one keeps, observe the means one employs to achieve certain ends, and understand what one is content with and what one is discontent with. How can one conceal his character? How can one conceal his character?"

2

Ziyou said, "Being overly meticulous in serving the prince will cause disgrace; being overly meticulous in dealing with friends will lead to estrangement."

四 三

子曰：『晏平仲善與人交，久而敬之。』

二

子曰：『巧言、令色、足恭，左丘明恥之，丘亦恥之。匿怨而友其人，左丘明恥之，丘亦恥之。』

一

子曰：『三人行，必有我師焉，擇其善者而從之，其不善者而改之。』

3

Confucius said, "Yan Pingzhong was good at getting along with people. The longer the people have known him, the more they have respected him."

Confucius said, "Flowery words, hypocritical appearance, and excessive deference—Zuo Qiuming was ashamed of them, and I am also ashamed of them. To conceal resentment against a person and appear friendly with him—Zuo Qiuming was ashamed of this conduct, and I am also ashamed of it."

4

Confucius said, "When I walk in a group of people, there must be one I can learn from. I would choose their merits to follow and their imperfections to correct."

五
〓

子曰：『可與共學，未可與適道；可與適道，未可與立；可與立，未可與權。』

六
〓

朋友死，無所歸，曰：『於我殯。』

朋友之饋，雖車馬，非祭肉，不拜。

5

Confucius said, "Those who can study with you may not necessarily be able to achieve something together with you. Those who can achieve something with you may not necessarily be able to act according to propriety in all things with you. And those who can act according to propriety in all things with you may not necessarily be able to adapt to changing circumstances together with you."

6

When a friend died without anyone to take charge of the burial, Confucius said, "I will take care of the funeral arrangements."

Upon receiving a gift from friends, even though it may be as expensive as a carriage and horses, Confucius would not perform the ritual of gratitude unless it was sacrificial meat.

七

二

子貢問友。子曰：『忠告而善道之，不可則止，毋自辱焉。』

曾子曰：『君子以文會友，以友輔仁。』

7

Zigong asked about friendship. Confucius said, "Advise them sincerely and guide them properly. If they are unwilling to listen, then stop. Do not humiliate yourself."

Zengzi said, "The gentleman makes friends through his literary talents and learning. This friendship enables him to cultivate his own virtue."

八

二一

子曰：『躬自厚而薄責於人，則遠怨矣。』

子曰：『羣居終日，言不及義，好行小慧，難矣哉！』

子曰：『君子矜而不爭，羣而不黨。』

子曰：『道不同，不相爲謀。』

8

Confucius said, "If one is severe with himself and is lenient towards others, he will keep resentment away."

Confucius said, "It is difficult to instruct those who gather together all day long chatting about everything except for righteousness and boasting about some shallow wisdom!"

Confucius said, "The gentleman is dignified and magnanimous without engaging in disputes, and sociable without forming cliques."

Confucius said, "Those who have different principles do not seek advice from one another."

十 九

孔子曰：『益者三友，損者三友。友直，友諒，友多聞，益矣。友便辟，友善柔，友便佞，損矣。』

孔子曰：『見善如不及，見不善如探湯。吾見其人矣，吾聞其語矣。隱居以求其志，行義以達其道。吾聞其語矣，未見其人也』。

9

Confucius said, "There are three types of beneficial friends and three types of harmful friends. It is beneficial to associate with those who are upright, trustworthy, and broad-minded. It is harmful to associate with those who are sycophantic, who flatter openly but slander behind your back, and who boast without substance."

10

Confucius said, " 'Seeing goodness and pursuing it as if they would never be able to achieve it; seeing badness and recoiling from it as if they have been scalded by boiling water.'—I have seen such people and I have heard such a saying. 'Living in seclusion to pursue their aspirations, and practicing righteousness to carry out their principles.'—I have heard such a saying, but I have never seen such people."

第

八

章

Chapter VIII   Conduct

行

一

子夏曰：『賢賢易色；事父母，能竭其力；事君，能致其身；與朋友交，言而有信。雖曰未學，吾必謂之學矣。』

二

子曰：『放於利而行，多怨。』

子曰：『君子欲訥於言，而敏於行。』

1

Zixia said, "One should pay attention to his wife's inner qualities and virtues rather than her outward appearance. When serving parents, one should exercise himself to the fullest. When serving one's prince, one should be willing to sacrifice his life. When interacting with friends, one should be sincere, earnest and truthful. I regard such one as well-educated and cultivated even though he may not have any formal education."

2

Confucius said, "Those who act out of self-interest will cause much resentment from others."

Confucius said, "The gentleman should be cautious and deliberate in speech, but diligent and prompt in action."

三

季文子三思而後行。子聞之，曰：『再，斯可矣。』

宰予晝寢。子曰：『朽木不可雕也，糞土之牆不可杇也；於予與何誅？』

子曰：『始吾於人也，聽其言而信其行；今吾於人也，聽其言而觀其行。於予與改是。』

3

Ji Wenzi always contemplated multiple times before taking action. When Confucius heard this, he said, "Twice would be enough for deliberation."

Zai Yu was sleeping in broad daylight. Confucius said, "Rotten wood cannot be carved; a wall of mud and dung is beyond plastering. What is the point of scolding Zai Yu?"

Confucius said, "Formerly, in my relationship with people, after I'd heard what they said, I trusted what they did. But now I listen to what a man says and observe what he would do accordingly. It was on account of Zai Yu that I made this change."

四
二

仲弓問子桑伯子。子曰：『可也簡。』

仲弓曰：『居敬而行簡，以臨其民，不亦可乎？居簡而行簡，無乃大簡乎？』子曰：『雍之言然。』

五
二

子曰：『蓋有不知而作之者，我無是也。多聞，擇其善者而從之；多見而識之；知之次也。』

子曰：『文莫吾猶人也。躬行君子，則吾未之有得。』

子曰：『君子坦蕩蕩，小人長戚戚。』

4

Zhonggong asked about Zisang Bozi. Confucius said, "He is all right in his simple approach."

Zhonggong said, "If one approaches things with sincerity and seriousness, and applies simplicity in governance, is it not possible to govern the people well? But if one approaches things with simplicity and take simple measures in governance, would that not be too simplistic?" Confucius said, "Your words are correct."

5

Confucius said, "There are probably those who know nothing yet fabricate knowledge out of thin air, but I am certainly not one of them. I listen extensively and choose what is good to follow. I observe attentively and learn things by heart. Knowledge gained this way is second only to innate knowledge."

Confucius said, "In terms of book knowledge, perhaps I am equal to others. But as for practicing to be a true gentleman in daily life, I have not yet succeeded."

Confucius said, "The gentleman is broad-minded, and always at ease, whereas the petty man is narrow-minded, full of distress."

六

二一

子曰：『其身正，不令而行；其身不正，雖令不從。』

子曰：『苟正其身矣，於從政乎何有？不能正其身，如正人何？』

6

Confucius said, "When a prince is upright, things will go smoothly even though no orders have been issued. But if he is not upright, the people will not obey even if he has issued repeated orders."

Confucius said, "If one sets himself correct, what difficulties will he have in governing the state? But if one cannot rectify himself, how can he guide others along the right path?"

七

子貢問曰：『何如斯可謂之士矣？』子曰：『行己有恥，使於四方，不辱君命，可謂士矣。』

曰：『敢問其次。』曰：『宗族稱孝焉，鄉黨稱弟焉。』

曰：『敢問其次。』曰：『言必信，行必果，硜硜然小人哉！抑亦可以爲次矣。』

子曰：『不得中行而與之，必也狂狷乎！狂者進取，狷者有所不爲也。』

7

Zigong asked, "What makes a person a true scholar-official?" Confucius said, "A person who maintains a sense of humility and fulfills the tasks of his prince when sent on missions abroad can be called a true scholar-official."

Zigong asked, "May I ask what kind of person ranks one step below that?" Confucius said, "One who is praised by his clan for being filial to his parents and by his neighborhood for being respectful to his elders."

Zigong asked again, "May I ask what kind of person may be placed in the next lower rank?" Confucius said, "A person whose word can be trusted and who completes whatever task he undertakes. In his stubborn determination, he may resemble a petty man, and he could still probably qualify as a scholar-official of a lower rank."

Confucius said, "If I cannot find people who are moderate in speech and action to associate with, I must relate myself to the fervent and the prudent. The fervent will press forward with determination, and the prudent will refrain from doing evil."

八一

子張問行。子曰：『言忠信，行篤敬，雖蠻貊之邦行矣。言不忠信，行不篤敬，雖州里行乎哉？立則見其參於前也，在輿則見其倚於衡也，夫然後行。』子張書諸紳。

子貢問曰：『有一言而可以終身行之者乎？』子曰：『其恕乎！己所不欲，勿施於人。』

8

Zizhang asked how one could conduct oneself so as to be successful everywhere. Confucius said, "If one speaks sincerely and honestly and behaves with integrity and dignity, even in a foreign land, one will succeed. But if one speaks deceitfully and behaves harshly and flippantly, even in one's own hometown, how can one succeed? When standing, one should imagine seeing the words 'sincerity, honesty, integrity, and dignity' before one's eyes; in the carriage, one should imagine seeing these words carved on the front beam. Only by constantly keeping these words in mind can one succeed everywhere." Zizhang wrote these words on his sash.

Zigong asked, "Is there a single word that can serve as a lifetime guide?" Confucius replied, "Perhaps it is 'empathy'. Do not impose on others what you do not desire for yourself."

九

子曰：『由也！女聞六言六蔽矣乎？』對曰：『未也。』

『居！吾語女：好仁不好學，其蔽也愚；好知不好學，其蔽也蕩；好信不好學，其蔽也賊；好直不好學，其蔽也絞；好勇不好學，其蔽也亂；好剛不好學，其蔽也狂。』

子曰：『小子何莫學夫詩？詩，可以興，可以觀，可以羣，可以怨。邇之事父，遠之事君，多識於鳥獸草木之名。』

9

Confucius asked Zilu, "Have you heard that a man of six virtues may be bewildered and beclouded if he does not study?" Zilu answered, "No, I have not."

Confucius said, "Sit down, and I will tell you why. If you love humaneness but do not like to study, you will be vulnerable to deception. If you love wisdom but do not like to study, you will be vulnerable to sensual indulgences. If you love trustworthiness but do not like to study, you will be vulnerable to harm. If you love directness but do not like to study, you will become a man of harsh words. If you love bravery but do not like to study, you will be rebellious. If you love resoluteness but do not like to study, you will be audacious."

Confucius said, "Young men, why do you not study the *Book of Songs*? The *Book of Songs* can enrich your imagination, provide a vehicle for contemplation, help you to interact with others, and voice a complaint more effectively. At home it teaches you how to serve your parents; further afield it teaches you how to serve the prince. Additionally, it helps you gain knowledge of birds, beasts, plants and trees."

十二

子曰：『不降其志，不辱其身，伯夷、叔齊與！』謂『柳下惠、少連，降志辱身矣，言中倫，行中慮，其斯而已矣』。

10

Confucius said, "Those who refused to change their mind or disgrace themselves were Boyi and Shuqi." He continued, "Liuxia Hui and Shao Lian surrendered their wills and disgraced themselves, but their words were morally sound and they thought before acting. That is all that can be said of the two."

第

九

章

Chapter IX　Gentleman

君
子

一

二

子曰：『君子不器。』

子貢問君子。子曰：『先行其言而後從之。』

子曰：『君子周而不比，小人比而不周。』

1

Confucius said, "The gentleman is not like a utensil that is limited to a specific use."

Zigong asked about the qualities of the gentleman. Confucius said, "First accomplish what you want to say and then say it. That is enough to be called a gentleman."

Confucius said, "The gentleman unites and does not plot with others; the petty man plots and does not unite with others."

二

子曰：『質勝文則野，文勝質則史。文質彬彬，然後君子。』

子曰：『君子博學於文，約之以禮，亦可以弗畔矣夫！』

三

棘子成曰：『君子質而已矣，何以文爲？』子貢曰：『惜乎！夫子之說君子也，駟不及舌。文猶質也，質猶文也。虎豹之鞟，猶犬羊之鞟。』

子曰：『君子成人之美，不成人之惡。小人反是。』

2

Confucius said, "Too much simplicity without sufficient ornament leads to coarseness, while too much ornament without sufficient simplicity leads to superficiality. It is the proper balance between ornament and simplicity that makes a true gentleman."

Confucius said, "The gentleman extensively studies the classics and then restrains himself with propriety, thereby avoiding deviation from the path of righteousness."

3

Ji Zicheng said, "The gentleman only needs to have a good nature; what need is there for refinement, such as propriety and formality?" Zigong replied, "I am sorry to say that you have spoken wrongly about the gentleman. Once words are uttered, they cannot be easily retrieved. Both nature and refinement are equally important. When the ornamental fur is taken off the hide of a tiger or leopard, it looks the same as the hide of a dog or sheep."

Confucius said, "The gentleman helps others to accomplish good deeds and does not assist in their wrongdoings. The petty man does the opposite."

四

二

司馬牛問君子。子曰：『君子不憂不懼。』

曰：『不憂不懼，斯謂之君子已乎？』子曰：『內省不疚，夫何憂何懼？』

司馬牛憂曰：『人皆有兄弟，我獨無。』子夏曰：『商聞之矣：死生有命，富貴在天。君子敬而無失，與人恭而有禮，四海之內皆兄弟也，君子何患乎無兄弟也？』

4

Sima Niu asked about the qualities of the gentleman. Confucius said, "The gentleman does not worry or fear."

Sima Niu said, "How can one be a gentleman when he does not worry or fear?" Confucius replied, "If one is without guilt in his heart, what is there to worry or fear about?"

Sima Niu said sorrowfully, "Others all have good brothers, but I alone have none." Zixia replied, "I have heard that life and death are determined by fate, and wealth and eminence rest with Heaven. The gentleman only needs to be diligent and careful in his work, and to be respectful and polite in his dealings with others. Within the Four Seas all men are brothers. Why should the gentleman worry about not having good brothers?"

五

二

子路問君子。子曰：『修己以敬。』

曰：『如斯而已乎？』曰：『修己以安人。』

曰：『如斯而已乎？』曰：『修己以安百姓。修己以安百姓，堯、舜其猶

病諸！』

5

Zilu asked about the qualities of the gentleman. Confucius said, "Cultivate yourself to be diligent and serious in your work."

Zilu asked, "Is that enough?" Confucius replied, "Cultivate yourself so that those in high positions are at ease."

Zilu asked again, "Is that all?" Confucius answered, "Cultivate yourself so that all the common people are at ease. Even Yao and Shun, the legendary emperors of ancient times, probably did not fully achieve cultivating themselves to ensure the well-being of all the common people."

六二

子曰：『君子義以爲質，禮以行之，孫以出之，信以成之。君子哉！』

子曰：『君子病無能焉，不病人之不己知也。』

子曰：『君子疾沒世而名不稱焉。』

子曰：『君子求諸己，小人求諸人。』

子曰：『君子矜而不爭，羣而不黨。』

6

Confucius said, "The gentleman in his endeavors takes righteousness as the fundamental principle, carries it out according to propriety, expresses it with modest words, and accomplishes it with a sincere attitude. Such is a gentleman indeed!"

Confucius said, "The gentleman is only ashamed of his own incompetence and does not resent being unrecognized by others."

Confucius said, "The gentleman considers it a regret if his name is not remembered and spoken of after his death."

Confucius said, "The gentleman makes demands on himself. The petty man makes demands on others."

Confucius said, "The gentleman is dignified and magnanimous without engaging in disputes, and sociable without forming cliques."

子曰：『君子不以言舉人，不以人廢言。』

子曰：『君子謀道不謀食。耕也，餒在其中矣；學也，祿在其中矣。君子憂道不憂貧。』

子曰：『君子不可小知，而可大受也；小人不可大受，而可小知也。』

子曰：『君子貞而不諒。』

Confucius said, "The gentleman does not promote a person simply because of his good words, nor does he disregard good words just because they come from a wicked person."

Confucius said, "The gentleman is devoted to seeking the Way, not a living. When farming, he often goes hungry; but in learning, he often receives remuneration. The gentleman is concerned about the Way, not about avoiding poverty."

Confucius said, "The gentleman should not be tested with trivial matters but can be entrusted with important commissions; the petty man should not undertake important tasks but can be tested with trivial matters."

Confucius said, "The gentleman is firmly upright but not obstinately truthful."

七

二

孔子曰：『君子有三戒：少之時，血氣未定，戒之在色；及其壯也，血氣方剛，戒之在鬥；及其老也，血氣既衰，戒之在得。』

孔子曰：『君子有三畏：畏天命，畏大人，畏聖人之言。小人不知天命而不畏也，狎大人，侮聖人之言。』

7

Confucius said, "The gentleman should be wary of three things: In youth, when his vital energies are not yet settled, he must be on guard against infatuation with women; when he reaches maturity, and his vital energies are strong, he must be on guard against combative pride; and in old age, when his vital energies have waned, he must be on guard against insatiable greed."

Confucius said, "The gentleman stands in awe of three things: the Mandate of Heaven, great men and the words of sages. The petty man, not knowing the Mandate of Heaven, is unafraid of it. He belittles great men, and he regards the words of sages with mockery."

九　八

八

孔子曰：『君子有九思：視思明，聽思聰，色思溫，貌思恭，言思忠，事思敬，疑思問，忿思難，見得思義。』

九

子夏曰：『雖小道，必有可觀者焉；致遠恐泥，是以君子不爲也。』

子夏曰：『百工居肆以成其事，君子學以致其道。』

8

Confucius said, "There are nine things the gentleman gives thought to: he aims to be clear in vision, keen in hearing, amicable in his expression, courteous in his manners, conscientious in carrying out his words, and respectful in attending to his responsibilities; and when encountering doubts, he considers how to seek advice from others; when becoming angry, he considers the possible consequences; when seeing something desirable, he considers whether it is right for him to obtain it."

9

Zixia said, "Even in small crafts, there must be something worth seeing; however, pursuing them to the extreme might be a hindrance to great causes, which is why the gentleman does not engage in them."

Zixia said, "The various craftsmen reside in their workshops to complete their work, while the gentleman approaches the Way through learning."

十二

十一

子夏曰：『君子有三變：望之儼然，卽之也溫，聽其言也厲。』

子夏曰：『君子信而後勞其民；未信，則以爲厲己也。信而後諫；未信，則以爲謗己也。』

子貢曰：『君子之過也，如日月之食焉：過也，人皆見之；更也，人皆仰之。』

10

Zixia said, "The gentleman presents himself in different ways: When viewed from afar, he appears solemn and awe-inspiring; when approached, he is gentle and amiable; when heard speaking, he is determined and strict."

Zixia said, "The gentleman must first gain the trust of the people before mobilizing them; otherwise, the people will think he is oppressing them. He must earn the trust of the prince before offering advice; otherwise, the prince will interpret it as defamation."

Zigong said, "The mistakes of the gentleman are like the eclipses of the sun and the moon. When he makes a mistake, everyone sees it; when he corrects it, everyone looks up to him."

第十章

章

Chapter X   Governance

爲政

一

子曰：『爲政以德，譬如北辰，居其所而衆星共之。』

二

子貢問政。子曰：『足食，足兵，民信之矣。』

子貢曰：『必不得已而去，於斯三者何先？』曰：『去兵。』

子貢曰：『必不得已而去，於斯二者何先？』曰：『去食。自古皆有死，

民無信不立。』

1

Confucius said, "When one governs a state with virtue, one will be like the North Star, standing in its place with all the other stars revolving around it."

2

Zigong asked about governance. Confucius said, "Sufficient food, sufficient weapons, and faith of the people."

Zigong asked, "If obliged to do away with one of these three, which should go first?" Confucius replied, "Weapons."

Zigong again asked, "Which of the two remaining may be dispensed with if obliged to?" Confucius answered, "Food. Death has been the human lot since time immemorial. However, without the faith of the people, a state cannot stand firm."

齊景公問政於孔子。孔子對曰：『君君，臣臣，父父，子子。』公曰：『善哉！信如君不君，臣不臣，父不父，子不子，雖有粟，吾得而食諸？』

子張問政。子曰：『居之無倦，行之以忠。』

季康子問政於孔子。孔子對曰：『政者，正也。子帥以正，孰敢不正？』

季康子問政於孔子曰：『如殺無道，以就有道，何如？』

孔子對曰：『子爲政，焉用殺？子欲善而民善矣。君子之德風，小人之德草。草上之風，必偃。』

Prince Jing of Qi asked Confucius about governance. Confucius replied, "The prince should be prince, embodying true virtue; the minister should be minister, embodying perfect deference; the father should be father, embodying love and kindness, and the son should be son, embodying filial piety." Prince Jing said, "How true! When the prince does not act like a prince, the minister not a minister, the father not a father, and the son not a son, even if I have plenty of food, can I enjoy it?"

Zizhang asked about governance. Confucius said, "Execute the responsibilities of your office tirelessly. Carry out your duties faithfully."

Ji Kangzi asked Confucius about governance. Confucius said, "To 'govern' means 'to be upright'. If you take the lead in being upright, who would dare not to follow suit?"

Ji Kangzi asked Confucius about governance, saying, "What would you think if I were to kill the wicked to get closer to the good people?"

Confucius replied, "Why do you resort to killing in governing? If you desire goodness, the people will naturally become good. The virtue of those at the top is like the wind; the virtue of the common people is like the grass. When the wind blows, the grass will surely bend."

三二

子路問政。子曰：『先之勞之。』請益。曰：『無倦。』

仲弓為季氏宰，問政。子曰：『先有司，赦小過，舉賢才。』曰：『焉知賢才而舉之？』曰：『舉爾所知。爾所不知，人其舍諸？』

3

Zilu asked about governance. Confucius said, "Take the lead, and then put the people to work." Zilu requested further elaboration, and Confucius added, "Never slack off."

Zhonggong, after being appointed as the steward for the Ji family, asked Confucius about governance. Confucius said, "Work hard and set an example for your subordinates, overlook their minor faults, and promote people of talent." Zhonggong asked, "How do I recognize that someone has talent and deserves to be promoted?" Confucius replied, "Promote those you recognize to be outstanding. As for those that you miss, will other people let them slip by you?"

四

子路曰：『衛君待子而爲政，子將奚先？』

子曰：『必也正名乎！』

子路曰：『有是哉，子之迂也！奚其正？』

子曰：『野哉由也！君子於其所不知，蓋闕如也。名不正，則言不順；言不順，則事不成；事不成，則禮樂不興；禮樂不興，則刑罰不中；刑罰不中，則民無所措手足。故君子名之必可言也，言之必可行也。君子於其言，無所苟而已矣。』

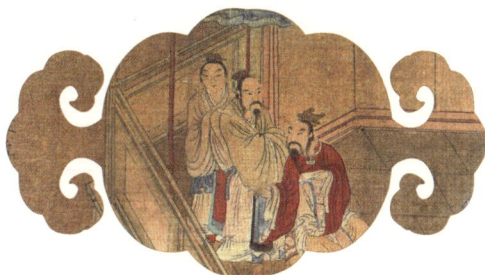

4

Zilu asked Confucius, "The Prince of Wei is anticipating your assistance in the governance of his state. What would you do first?"

Confucius answered, "It must be to correct the improper use of names."

Zilu asked, "Have you become so impractical? Why bother to correct them?"

Confucius replied, "How can you be so reckless! The gentleman is always cautious about things that he does not know. Improper use of names leads to disordered reasoning; disordered reasoning undermines effective action; ineffective action disrupts the Rites and Music; disrupted Rites and Music lead to improper punishments; improper punishments cause people to feel unsettled and unsure how to behave. Therefore, when the gentleman names something, the name can surely be well-reasoned; when he says something, his words can surely be carried out in action. When the gentleman speaks, there is nothing casual or careless about what he says."

五

二

樊遲請學稼。子曰：『吾不如老農。』

請學爲圃。曰：『吾不如老圃。』

樊遲出。子曰：『小人哉，樊須也！上好禮，則民莫敢不敬；上好義，

則民莫敢不服；上好信，則民莫敢不用情。夫如是，則四方之民，襁負

其子而至矣，焉用稼？』

子適衛，冉有僕。子曰：『庶矣哉！』冉有曰：『既庶矣，又何加焉？』

曰：『富之。』曰：『既富矣，又何加焉？』曰：『教之。』

5

Fan Chi asked to learn about farming grain. Confucius said, "An old farmer would be a better person to ask."

Fan Chi then asked to learn about growing vegetables. Confucius said, "An old gardener would be a better person to ask."

After Fan Chi left, Confucius said, "Fan Chi is truly a simple-minded person! When a ruler observes the Rites, the common people will respect him; if the ruler acts righteously, the common people will submit to him; if the ruler is sincere and trustworthy, the common people will speak the truth. If this is achieved, the people from all directions will come with their babies strapped to their backs. Why should he personally engage in farming?"

Confucius went to the State of Wei, with Ran You driving the carriage for him. Confucius remarked, "How populous it is here!" Ran You asked, "Now that the population is already large, what else needs to be done?" Confucius replied, "Enrich them." Ran You followed up, "What more needs to be done when they become rich?" Confucius said, "Educate them."

六

定公問：『一言而可以興邦，有諸？』

孔子對曰：『言不可以若是，其幾也。人之言曰：「爲君難，爲臣不易。」如知爲君之難也，不幾乎一言而興邦乎？』

曰：『一言而喪邦，有諸？』孔子對曰：『言不可以若是，其幾也。人之言曰：「予無樂乎爲君，唯其言而莫予違也。」如其善而莫之違也，不亦善乎？如不善而莫之違也，不幾乎一言而喪邦乎？』

6

Prince Ding of Lu asked, "Is there a saying that can make a state prosperous?"

Confucius replied, "Words cannot be taken so simply and mechanically. Nonetheless, people often say, 'Being a ruler is difficult, and being a minister is not easy.' If a ruler is fully aware of the challenging nature of his position, he will naturally be cautious and diligent. Would it not come close to having a saying that can make a state prosperous?"

Prince Ding asked further, "Is there a saying that can ruin a state?" Confucius replied, "Words cannot be taken so simply and mechanically. However, people often say, 'As a ruler, I have no other joy than that my words are not opposed.' If what the ruler says is correct and no one goes against him, is this not good? But if what the ruler says is incorrect and no one goes against him, would it not come close to having a saying that can ruin a state?"

七

子夏爲莒父宰，問政。子曰：『無欲速，無見小利。欲速，則不達；見小利，則大事不成。』

八

子曰：『無爲而治者，其舜也與？夫何爲哉？恭己正南面而已矣。』

7

When Zixia became the magistrate of Jufu, he asked Confucius about governance. Confucius said, "Do not wish for quick results, nor look for small gains; if you seek quick results, you will not achieve the ultimate goal; if you are led astray by small gains, you will never accomplish great things."

8

Confucius said, "Shun may be the only one who was able to govern efficiently without taking any deliberate action. What did he actually do? He did nothing but sit on his royal seat regally and majestically."

顏淵問爲邦。子曰：『行夏之時，乘殷之輅，服周之冕，樂則《韶》《舞》。放鄭聲，遠佞人。鄭聲淫，佞人殆。』

子張問於孔子曰：『何如斯可以從政矣？』

子曰：『尊五美，屏四惡，斯可以從政矣。』

子張曰：『何謂五美？』

子曰：『君子惠而不費，勞而不怨，欲而不貪，泰而不驕，威而不猛。』

子張曰：『何謂惠而不費？』

9

Yan Yuan asked about how to govern a state. Confucius said, "Observe the calendar of the Xia Dynasty, ride in the carriage of the Shang Dynasty, wear the ceremonial cap of the Zhou Dynasty. As for music, embrace the music of Shao and Wu. Discard the tunes of Zheng and keep at a distance from flatterers. The tunes of Zheng are decadent and obscene, and flatterers are dangerous."

10

Zizhang asked Confucius, "How can one govern effectively?"

Confucius replied, "By upholding Five Virtues and eliminating Four Vices, one can govern effectively."

Zizhang asked, "What are the Five Virtues?"

Confucius replied, "The gentleman blesses the people with happiness and prosperity without lavish spending; he labors the people without causing resentment; he focuses on pursuing the virtuous and the righteous without any interest in personal gain; he is dignified and composed without being arrogant; he is stern but not fierce."

Zizhang asked, "How can one bless the people without lavish spending?"

子曰：『因民之所利而利之，斯不亦惠而不費乎？擇可勞而勞之，又誰怨？欲仁而得仁，又焉貪？君子無衆寡，無小大，無敢慢，斯不亦泰而不驕乎？君子正其衣冠，尊其瞻視，儼然人望而畏之，斯不亦威而不猛乎？』

子張曰：『何謂四惡？』

子曰：『不教而殺謂之虐，不戒視成謂之暴，慢令致期謂之賊，猶之與人也，出納之吝，謂之有司。』

Confucius explained, "Encourage the people to engage in doing whatever would benefit themselves—is that not blessing the people without lavish spending? Choose appropriate times and conducive situations for the people to work—who would resent it? Desire righteousness and attain it—what more is there to covet? The gentleman dares not be disrespectful whether he is dealing with a few or with many, with people big or small—is that being dignified and composed without being arrogant? When the gentleman dresses neatly and avoids looking askance, commanding respect with solemnity—is that being stern without being fierce?"

Zizhang asked, "What are the Four Vices?"

Confucius replied, "Killing without educating is called cruelty; demanding results without warning is called tyranny; suddenly setting deadlines after initial laxity is called treachery; giving away wealth begrudgingly is called miserliness."